35 Money Skills Workbook for Teenagers Ages 15-19

Packed with Fun Challenges to Help You Master Budgeting, Grow Your Savings, Build Wealth, and Start Investing—Designed for Teens and First-Time Money Makers!

by Chad K. Smith, MBA

CONTENTS

INTRODUCTION

Learning how money works as a teen is one of the smartest moves you can make. Whether you're earning cash from babysitting, mowing lawns, or getting an allowance, this is only the beginning of your financial journey. The sooner you master earning, saving, investing, and managing your money, the faster you'll build absolute financial freedom—and this workbook is your playbook to make it happen. Inside, you'll find hands-on tools, challenges, and activities that help you take control of your money, boost your confidence, and set you up for life.

Making money as a teenager isn't just about having spending money for the weekend, it's about building responsibility and gaining the skills to succeed for life. Your first jobs teach you how to manage your time, hustle, and work hard. But here's what's even more exciting: you can think like an entrepreneur, solve real problems, and use your creativity to make money grow. Try teaming up with a friend or your crew and use this workbook together—you'll share ideas, help each other, and build even bigger wins.

Investing isn't just for adults. It's about making your money work for you. While savings accounts help you stack cash, investing helps it multiply. You'll learn how to run investment simulations, figure out your risk style, and build a practice portfolio that gets you ready for the real world. The earlier you start, the more your money can grow.

Saving money might not sound exciting, but it's a total game-changer. Even setting aside a little bit from each paycheck gives you freedom and options—like saving for a car, college, or an epic trip. With this workbook, you'll use easy tools and goal-setting strategies to turn saving into a habit. Before you know it, you'll be in charge of your money instead of the other way around.

Debt doesn't have to be scary if you know how to handle it. You'll learn how to avoid traps, make wise choices with credit cards or student loans, and pay off what you owe without stress. Building these habits early means you'll be ready for anything.

Budgeting is your secret weapon. It's not about cutting out everything fun, it's about making sure your money goes where you want it to. You'll create your budget, learn to handle ups and downs in your income, and still enjoy what you love.

Protecting what you earn matters, too. You'll pick up pro tips on keeping your money safe, planning, and learning innovative tax strategies. These topics might sound grown-up, but knowing them now means you'll be way ahead of the game.

You're growing up in a world where technology is changing money every day. That's why getting savvy with fintech tools, savings apps, and even learning a bit about blockchain will set you apart. This workbook will show you how to manage your cash in a digital world, track your spending in real time, and use apps to make life easier and smarter.

Every page in this workbook is a step toward building real wealth. From your first paycheck to your first investments, you'll see how money can work for you. And once you discover the power of compound interest, you'll never want to put off saving or reinvesting. (Trust me, look it up—it's wild!)

Finishing this workbook is just your starting line. Keep practicing, keep learning, and keep making wise choices because every new skill brings you closer to the life you want! You're not just learning about money—you're creating a future you'll be proud to show off!

Let's get this party started!

📣 WHY THIS WORKBOOK MATTERS—PARENTS AND EDUCATORS

- 🎯 Builds real-world skills in saving, investing, budgeting, and entrepreneurship
- 💬 Encourages open, empowering family conversations about money
- 🛠️ Equips teens with lifelong habits for financial confidence and independence
- 📚 Reinforces classroom learning with hands-on activities and practical applications

- Sparks critical thinking and decision-making in real-life money scenarios
- Promotes financial literacy through tech tools and modern innovations teens already use
- Fosters responsibility, discipline, and a growth mindset in young learners

INTRODUCTION (CONT.)

Objective: Understand the basic concepts of personal finance and begin to adopt a growth mindset toward wealth building.

Activity: Reflect on your current financial mindset and goals. Write a short essay (1–2 pages) about your current financial habits, beliefs, and what you hope to achieve by completing this workbook. Please try your best!

CHAPTER 1

SIMPLIFYING FINANCIAL TERMS AND INVESTMENT BASICS

Objective: Gain a fundamental knowledge of financial terms to improve understanding and serve as a reference.

ACTIVITY 1: FINANCIAL GLOSSARY CREATION CHALLENGE

Term	Definition	Example	Notes/Updates
X	*Write the term's definition in your own words*	*Provide an example of how this term applies in the real world*	*Add any additional notes or updates as you learn more*

Challenge yourself to create a glossary of financial terms introduced in this workbook. Writing things down helps you learn! Include definitions and examples in your own words. Knowledge is your inner strength, so update it as you progress!

Term	Definition	Example	Notes/Updates

Term	Definition	Example	Notes/Updates

FINANCIAL DEFINITIONS

Assets – Items of value you own, such as cash, property, or investments.
Blockchain – A decentralized digital ledger used to record transactions securely across many computers.
Budgeting – Creating a financial plan to manage income and expenses, helping you save and avoid debt.
Capital Gains – The profit from the sale of an asset such as stocks or real estate.
Compound Interest – The interest on a loan or deposit calculated based on both the initial principal and the accumulated interest from previous periods.
Credit Score – A number based on your credit files, representing your creditworthiness.
Cryptocurrency – A digital or virtual currency, such as Bitcoin, that uses cryptography for security.
Debt – Money owed to someone else, which can include loans, credit card balances, or mortgages.
Debt Reduction Strategy – A plan to lower and eliminate outstanding debts, such as paying off credit card balances.
Diversification – The practice of spreading investments across various financial instruments to reduce risk.
Dividend – A payment made by a corporation to its shareholders, usually as a distribution of profits.
Dollar- Cost Averaging – A strategy that involves regularly investing a fixed dollar amount in a particular investment, regardless of the share price.
Emergency Fund – Savings reserved for unexpected expenses (medical, repairs, etc.).
Entrepreneurship – The process of starting and operating your own business, taking on financial risks in the hope of profit.
Estate Planning – Arranging for the management and disposal of your estate after death, ensuring your assets go to the right people.
FICO Score – A type of credit score created by the Fair Isaac Corporation, used by lenders to assess credit risk. Assets or contracts that can be traded, such as stocks, bonds, mutual funds
Financial Instruments – Assets or contracts that can be traded, such as stocks, bonds, mutual funds, and savings accounts, which help people grow their money or protect their wealth.

Fintech (Financial Technology) – The integration of technology in financial services, such as apps for budgeting and investing.
401(k) – A retirement savings plan sponsored by an employer that allows workers to save and invest a portion of their paycheck before taxes are taken out.
GDP (Gross Domestic Product) – The total value of goods produced and services provided in a country during one year, often used as an indicator of economic health.
Gross Income – Your total earnings before any deductions such as taxes or retirement contributions.
Inflation – The rate at which the general level of prices for goods and services rises, eroding purchasing power.
Inflation Hedge – An investment that is considered to protect against the reduced purchasing power of money due to inflation, such as real estate or commodities.
Interest Rate – The percentage charged on a loan or earned on an investment.
Investing – Allocating money with the expectation of generating income or profit, typically in assets like stocks, bonds, or real estate.
IRA (Individual Retirement Account) – A savings account with tax advantages that individuals can use to save and invest for retirement.
Leverage – Using borrowed funds to increase the potential return on investment.
Liabilities – Financial obligations or debts that you owe.
Liquidity – The ease with which an asset can be converted into cash without affecting its market price.
Mutual Fund – A pool of money from many investors that is managed to buy a diversified portfolio of stocks, bonds, or other securities.
Net Income – Your total earnings after all deductions, representing your take-home pay.
Net Worth – The difference between your total assets and total liabilities.
Passive Income – Earnings derived from rental property, limited partnerships, or other enterprises in which the individual is not actively involved.
Philanthropy – The desire to promote the welfare of others, often through charitable donations and efforts.
Real Estate Investment Trust (REIT) – A company that owns, operates, or finances income-producing real estate, offering a way to invest in property without direct ownership.
Risk Tolerance – How much risk an investor can tolerate.
Roth IRA – An individual retirement account that allows after-tax contributions to grow tax-free and be withdrawn tax-free in retirement.
Savings – Money set aside for future use, often in a bank or other secure account.

SMART Goals – Specific, Measurable, Achievable, Relevant, and Time-bound goals used in financial planning and saving.
Stock Market – A public market for buying and selling stocks, where the value of companies is traded.
Tax- efficient Investing – Strategies that minimize taxes on investment returns.

ACTIVITY 2A: INVESTMENT PORTFOLIO SIMULATION—TIME TO TEST YOUR SKILLS!

Search for some online simulators or you can use "**Investopedia Simulator**" or "**Wall Street Survivor**" to simulate a basic investment portfolio. Allocate funds across stocks, bonds, and mutual funds based on the chart below. Track the performance over a simulated six-month period and record your observations each month.

6-Month Portfolio Allocation			
Asset Type	Initial Allocation (%)	Amount Invested ($)	Reason for Allocation
XXXX	*20 %*	*$ 10,000*	*Explain your rationale for this allocation based on your goals. Additional space below can be used for other assets like real estate, crypto, collector items, etc.*
Stocks			
Bonds			
Mutual Funds			
Total Investment	100 %	$	

Portfolio Performance Tracking					
Month	Stock(s)	Bond(s)	Mutual Fund(s)	Total Portfolio Value ($)	Observations
Month X	*$ 200*	*$ 300*	*$ 250*	*$ 750*	***Record any changes in portfolio value and reasons for those changes.***
Month 1	$	$	$	$	
Month 2	$	$	$	$	
Month 3	$	$	$	$	
Month 4	$	$	$	$	
Month 5	$	$	$	$	
Month 6	$	$	$	$	

SUMMARY OF OBSERVATIONS (DO THIS AFTER SIX MONTHS OF SIMULATION)

Overall Performance: Describe how your portfolio performed over the six-month period. Did it meet your expectations? Why or why not?

____

____

____

Risk-Reward Balance: Reflect on the risk-reward balance you chose. Was it appropriate for your investment goals? What would you change if you did this simulation again?

____

____

____

Lessons Learned: Summarize the key takeaways from this simulation. How might this exercise influence your real-life investment decisions?

____

____

____

ACTIVITY 2B: CREATE YOUR OWN VISION BOARD

A vision board is a visual tool that helps you clarify, concentrate on, and maintain focus on specific life goals and aspirations. To create one, gather images, quotes, and items that represent your goals, then arrange them on a board/poster or a digital image to create a visual representation of what you want to achieve. Ensure you put it someplace where you will see it every day, like your bathroom mirror or desktop computer, to keep you motivated and inspired!

ACTIVITY 3: IMPACT CHALLENGE: TEACH WHAT YOU JUST LEARNED

This challenge gives you the chance to become the teacher! After building your financial glossary, choose five important financial terms and explain them to someone else using your own words.

📝 **Instructions:** In your own words, write out the five terms from your glossary that interest you the most.

1. ______________________________

2. ______________________________

3. ______________________________

4. ______________________________

5. ______________________________

Find someone at home or school—a parent, sibling, or friend.

Teach them what each term means and how it could be used in everyday life.

🎯 **Objective:** Reinforce your knowledge by teaching others. It helps you retain the information better and builds confidence in talking about money.

📸 **Optional Action:** Take a photo of your completed glossary and send it to someone you trust (like a parent or teacher) with a message like: "Look what I've been learning about money!"

📣 **Challenge Extension:** Ask the person you taught to quiz you later this week. Teaching + review = mastery!

Reflection: How did it feel to explain financial terms to someone else? Which term did you find the easiest to explain? Which one was the hardest?

CHAPTER 2
CRAFTING A FOOLPROOF SAVING STRATEGY

Objective: Develop practical saving habits and a realistic budget tailored to your personal financial goals.

ACTIVITY 4: SMART FINANCIAL GOAL SETTING

Identify four financial goals using the SMART criteria (Specific, Measurable, Achievable, Relevant, Time-bound). Be creative! 😊

SMART Financial Goals (EXAMPLE)				
Goal	SMART Criteria	Steps to Achieve	Potential Challenges	Solutions/ Contingency Plans
Specific	(EXAMPLE) I want to save $500 in 5 months.	-Set aside $25 each week -Track Spending	-Spending $$ -Not having any income	-Use a budget app -Start a side hustle, babysitting, walking dogs, mow lawns, etc.
Measurable	How will you measure progress?	-Create a tracker to log weekly progress -Measure money weekly	-Not able to find work -Not saving enough	-Partner with others for accountability
Achievable	Is the goal realistic?	-Write out how I will find opportunities	-Not finding enough jobs	-Offer other services online or find what homeowners need in other neighborhoods
Relevant	How does this goal align with your overall financial objectives?	-Remind yourself about your "WHY" -Keep that vision board and flex when plans change	-Losing interest or comparing self with others who get things easily	-Focus on your independence -Find a mentor or a parent and discuss the issues, along with your thoughtful solutions
Time-bound	Set a deadline for achieving the goal.	-Set weekly and monthly milestones -Use a calendar to count progress	-Unexpected expenses or delays in earning money	-Build an emergency fund -Be flexible—plans change so keep moving forward

SMART Financial Goal 1				
Goal	SMART Criteria	Steps to Achieve	Potential Challenges	Solutions and Plans
Specific				
Measurable				
Achievable				
Relevant				
Time-bound				

SMART Financial Goal 2				
Goal	SMART Criteria	Steps to Achieve	Potential Challenges	Solutions and Plans
Specific				
Measurable				
Achievable				
Relevant				
Time-bound				

SMART Financial Goal 3				
Goal	SMART Criteria	Steps to Achieve	Potential Challenges	Solutions and Plans
Specific				
Measurable				
Achievable				
Relevant				
Time-bound				

SMART Financial Goal 4				
Goal	SMART Criteria	Steps to Achieve	Potential Challenges	Solutions and Plans
Specific				
Measurable				
Achievable				
Relevant				
Time-bound				

SUMMARY OF GOALS

When developing these goals, take some time to get more familiar with the term "compound interest." At least one of your goals must have the power to compound your investments!

Goal 1: [Writing out your goal helps you visualize your future. Do a nice summary below.]

____

____

____

Goal 2: [A written goal is a powerful step toward achievement. Briefly write it here.]

____

____

____

Goal 3: [Writing down your goals gives you clarity and purpose. Keep it simple and focused! Summarize it here.]

____

____

____

Goal 4: [Did you know goals in writing keep you motivated, accountable, and committed? Now, start self-disciplining toward success!]

____

____

____

ACTIVITY 5: PERSONALIZED BUDGET CREATION

Create a personalized budget using the 50/30/20 rule (50% is Your Needs; 30% is Your Wants; 20% is your Savings). List your income sources and categorize your expenses into needs, wants, and savings/debt repayment. Adjust the percentages based on your current financial situation and goals. Practice your discipline!

Expense Allocation Using 50/30/20 Rule		
Category	Target (%)	Monthly Budget ($)
Ex. Needs (50 %)	*50 %*	*$ 500*
Needs (50 %)	50 %	$
Wants (30 %)	30 %	$
Savings/Debt Repayments (20 %)	20 %	$

Needs		
Expenses	Monthly Amount ($)	Notes
(Example): Car	*$ 400*	*7th payment, $3,000 left to payoff*
1.	$	
2.	$	
3.	$	
4.	$	
5.	$	
6.	$	
7.	$	
8.	$	
9.	$	
Total Needs	$	

Wants		
Expense	Monthly Amount ($)	Notes
(Example) Netflix subscription	*$ 12*	*Potentially canceling this in May.*
1.	$	
2.	$	
3.	$	
4.	$	
5.	$	
6.	$	
7.	$	
8.	$	
9.	$	
Total Needs	$	

Savings/Debt Repayment		
Expense	Monthly Amount ($)	Notes
(Example) Emergency fund	*$ 500*	*E.g., emergency fund, loan payments*
Total Savings/Debt Repayment		

Adjustments and Reflection

Adjusting Percentages: If your current financial situation requires different percentages, record your adjustments here:

Needs: % ______________________________

Wants: % ______________________________

Savings/Debt Repayment: % ______________________

Reflection:

Are you comfortable with your current spending in each category? Why or why not?

____

____

____

What changes can you make to better align your spending with your financial goals?

____

____

____

How can you increase savings or reduce debt repayment time?

____

____

____

ACTIVITY 6: EMERGENCY FUND CALCULATION

Instructions: Calculate how much you need to save to build an emergency fund that covers three to six months of essential expenses. Develop a plan to achieve this target within a specified timeframe.

Step 1: *Identify Your Essential Monthly Expenses*

Instructions: List your essential monthly expenses below to calculate the total amount needed for your emergency fund.

Expense Category	Monthly Amount ($)
Housing (rent/mortgage)	*$500*
Entertainment	$
Phone	$
Groceries	$
Transportation	$
Hobbies	$
Debt Payments (minimum payments)	$
Other Essentials (e.g., medication)	$
Total Essential Monthly Expenses	$

Step 2: *Calculate Your Emergency Fund Target*

Instructions: Use the totals from Step 1 to calculate your emergency fund target for

both three and six months of expenses.

Three-month Emergency Fund:

- Calculation: Total Essential Monthly Expenses x 3
  - Amount Needed: $ ____________________

Six-Month Emergency Fund:

- Calculation: Total Essential Monthly Expenses x 6
  - Amount Needed: $ ____________________

***Step 3:** Develop a Savings Plan*

Instructions: Plan how much you need to save each month to reach your emergency fund goal within your desired timeframe.

Target Amount	Monthly Savings Goal ($)	Timeframe (Months)	Target Completion Date
3-Month Fund	*$500*	*3 Months*	*April 30, 20XX*
3-Month Fund	$ ______		
6-Month Fund	$ ______		

***Step 4:** Identify Strategies to Build Your Emergency Fund*

Instructions: List and describe strategies you will use to save for your emergency fund.

Strategy	Description	Estimated Monthly Contribution ($)
Automated Savings:	*Set up automatic transfers to a dedicated savings account.*	*$500*
Automated Savings:		$ ______
Cutting Non-Essential Expenses:		$ ______
Side Income:		$ ______
Selling Unused Items:		$ ______
Total Potential Contribution:		$ ______

Step 5: *Track Your Progress and Adjust as Needed*

Tracking:

- Set up a system to monitor your savings progress (e.g., using a spreadsheet or budgeting app).
- Schedule regular check-ins to ensure you are on track to meet your goal.

Adjustments:

- If you fall behind, identify ways to increase savings or reduce expenses.
- If your financial situation changes, update your plan accordingly.

Step 6: *Reflection*

Reflect on Your Progress:

Are you comfortable with the pace at which you're building your emergency fund? Why or why not?

____

____

____

What obstacles have you encountered, and how have you overcome them?

____

____

____

What could you do differently to accelerate your progress?

____

____

____

ACTIVITY 7: IMPACT CHALLENGE—HOST A MINI MONEY TALK AT HOME

Now it's time to show off your saving strategy and communication skills! Share what you've been working on by hosting a casual conversation with your family.

✏️ **Instructions:** Schedule a ten- to fifteen-minute "money talk" at dinner or any quiet time.

Walk them through:

- Your SMART Goals
- Your emergency fund plan
- Your budget (based on the 50/30/20 rule)

Ask: "What do you wish you knew about saving money when you were my age?"

🎯 **Objective:** Develop the confidence to speak about your financial goals and build family connection through shared learning.

📓 **Write It Down:** Record their response and advice in your journal or notebook. You might be surprised by their answer!

Reflection: What did you learn from your parent or guardian? Did they give you any saving tips you hadn't thought of before?

CHAPTER 3
ESSENTIALS OF INVESTING

Objective: Understand the basics of investing and develop a long-term investment strategy.

ACTIVITY 8: RISK PROFILE ASSESSMENT

Complete a risk profile questionnaire (you can find these online or in investing apps) to determine your risk tolerance. Use this information to inform your investment decisions.

Step 1: *Complete a Risk Profile Questionnaire*

Instructions: Search online or use an investing app to find a risk profile questionnaire. Complete the questionnaire to determine your risk tolerance. Record your results below.

Questionnaire Source	Date Completed	Risk Tolerance Score/Category
ABC	*Feb 8, 20XX*	*E.g., Conservative, Moderate, Aggressive*

Step 2: *Understanding Your Risk Profile*

Risk Tolerance Category	Description	Implications for Investment Decisions
Conservative	A conservative investor prioritizes capital preservation and is willing to accept lower returns for reduced risk.	Focus on low-risk investments like bonds, savings accounts, and dividend-paying stocks.
Moderate	A moderate investor is comfortable with some level of risk and volatility in exchange for potentially higher returns.	Mix of stocks, bonds, and possibly some real estate or mutual funds.
Aggressive	An aggressive investor is willing to take on high risk for the possibility of significant returns.	Focus on high-growth stocks, emerging markets, and other high-risk, high-reward investments.

Step 3: *Aligning Your Investment Strategy with Your Risk Profile*

Current Investment Strategy:

List your current investments and assess how they align with your risk tolerance.

Investment	Type (Stocks, Mutual Funds, Bonds, 401K, etc.)	Current Allocation (%)	vel (Low, Medium, High)
$500	*Stocks*	*15%*	*Medium*
$		%	
$		%	
$		%	
$		%	
$		%	
$		%	

Adjustments Based on Risk Profile:

Investment	Action (Increase, Decrease, Hold, Sell)	Reason
Bonds	*Decrease*	*E.g., increase allocation to stocks for higher returns.*

Identify any changes you need to make to better align your investments with your risk tolerance.

Step 4: *Reflection and Future Considerations*

Reflection on Risk Tolerance:

Does your risk profile align with your investment goals and financial situation? Why or why not?

____

____

____

How comfortable are you with the level of risk in your current investment portfolio? Do you think it should be adjusted according to your goals and plans? If so, act accordingly.

____

____

____

Future Considerations:

How might changes in your financial situation (e.g., income, expenses, life events) affect your risk tolerance? Remember, you must be flexible to adjust your finances. Ex: Since my money increased for the month, I added 10 percent more toward my savings.

____

____

____

What steps can you take to regularly reassess your risk profile and adjust your investment strategy accordingly? Note: You could write out your own personal checklist.

____

____

____

ACTIVITY 9: INVESTMENT STRATEGY PLAN

In this activity, you will learn to develop a personalized investment strategy that aligns with your risk profile, goals, and investment preferences.

Risk Profile Assessment

Describe Your Risk Tolerance:(e.g., conservative, moderate, aggressive)

____

____

____

Define Your Investment Goals

Instructions: Outline your short-term, medium-term, and long-term investment goals.

Investment Goal	Time Horizon	Target Amount ($)	Priority Level (High/Med./ Low)	Notes
Short-Term Goal:	*1-3 years*	*$ 1,500*	*High*	*Save for a car*
Short-Term Goal:	1-3 years	$________		
Medium-Term Goal:	3-7 years	$________		
Long-Term Goal:	7+ years	$________		

Reflection and Future Considerations

Reflection:

How comfortable are you with your current investment strategy? Do you need to do more research on your investments and other alternatives?

____

____

____

What challenges do you anticipate in sticking to your buy-and-hold and dollar-cost averaging strategies?

____

____

____

How might your investment strategy evolve as you approach your long-term goals?

____

____

____

Future Considerations:

As your financial situation or goals change, how will you adjust your asset allocation or investment approach?

____

____

____

How will you continue to educate yourself about investing to make informed decisions?

____

____

____

ACTIVITY 10: IMPACT CHALLENGE—BUILD A TEEN INVESTMENT PITCH

Here's your opportunity to present like a pro! Show that you've understood the fundamentals of investing by creating and delivering a simple pitch.

Instructions: Choose a simulated investment (e.g., stock, bond, or mutual fund).

Write down:

- What the investment is about
- Why you chose it (based on your risk profile)
- What return you are hoping for

Create a short, two-minute presentation or speech to give to your parent, sibling, or friend.

Optional Boost: Use a slideshow, poster, or drawing to support your explanation. Be creative!

Role-Playing Option: Pretend you're a stock advisor giving a tip to a client—what would you recommend and why?

Reflection: How did your audience react to your investment pitch? What feedback did you receive? Would you change anything about your approach?

CHAPTER 4
MANAGING DEBT AND BUDGETING EFFECTIVELY

Objective: Develop effective strategies to manage and reduce debt while maintaining a balanced budget.

ACTIVITY 11: DEBT REDUCTION STRATEGY WORKSHEET

Debt Type	Balance	Interest Rate (%)	Minimum Payment	Due Date
Borrowed Money from Family Member	*$ 2,000*	*10 %*	*$ 200*	Feb 17, 20XX
Family Loan	$_______	_____%	$_______	
Auto Loan	$_______	_____%	$_______	
Personal Loan	$_______	_____%	$_______	
	$_______	_____%	$_______	
	$_______	_____%	$_______	
	$_______	_____%	$_______	
	$_______	_____%	$_______	
	$_______	_____%	$_______	
	$_______	_____%	$_______	

List all your debts, including the interest rates and minimum payments. Choose between the Snowball and Avalanche methods for debt reduction and create a plan to pay off your debts systematically.

Choose Your Debt Reduction Method

Snowball Method:

Focus on paying off your smallest debt first while making minimum payments on the others. Once the smallest debt is paid off, move to the next smallest.

Avalanche Method:

Focus on paying off the debt with the highest interest rate first while making minimum payments on the others. Once the highest-interest debt is paid off, move to the next highest.

Chosen Method:

- ☐ Snowball
- ☐ Avalanche

Reason for Choice: ____

For Debt with Snowball Method (Smallest to Largest Balance):

Order #	Debt Type	Outstanding Balance ($)	Interest rate	Minimum Monthly Payments ($)
X	*Credit card*	*$ 500*	*14 %*	*50*
1				
2				
3				
4				
5				

For Debt with Avalanche Method (Highest to Lowest Interest Rate):

Order	Debt Type	Outstanding Balance ($)	Interest rate	Minimum Monthly Payments ($)
X	*Bank Loan*	*$ 20,000*	*25%*	*1,000*
1				
2				
3				
4				
5				

CREATING A DEBT REPAYMENT PLAN

Instructions: Determine how much you can contribute monthly toward debt

1. Calculate Total Minimum Monthly Payments: $________
2. Determine Extra Monthly Contribution: $________
3. Debt Repayment Schedule:

Apply the extra payment to the first debt on your list while making minimum payments on all others. Once the first debt is paid off, roll over its payment to the next debt.

Month	Debt Being Targeted	Minimum Payment ($)	Extra Payments($)	Total Payment ($)	Remaining Balance ($)
1	*Bank Loan*	*$ 1,000*	*$ 2,500*	*$ 3,500*	*$ 16,500*
1					
2					
3					
4					
5					

ACTIVITY 12: IRREGULAR INCOME BUDGETING

Objective: Create and adjust a budget tailored to an irregular income using income averaging or the envelope system. Track your income and expenses over three months to refine your budgeting approach.

1. Choose Your Budgeting System

Method Income Averaging:

- Calculate your average monthly income by looking at past earnings and use this figure to plan your budget.

Envelope System:

- Allocate cash to different spending categories (envelopes) based on your expected income. Spend only what is in each envelope.

Chosen Method:

☐ Income Averaging
☐ Envelope System

2. Track Your Income and Expenses

Step 1: Record your <u>income</u> for three months:

Month	Income Source	Amount Received	Total Income
Month X	*Primary Job*	*$ 1,500*	*$ 1,700*
Month 1			
Month 2			
Month 3			

Step 2: Record your <u>expenses</u> for three months:

Month	Category	Planned Expense	Actual Expense
Month X	*Groceries*	*$ 500*	*$ 800*
Month 1			
Month 2			
Month 3			

Step 3: Adjust Your Budget as Necessary Analysis:

- Compareyourincomeandexpensestoyourinitialbudget.Identifyany discrepancies.
- Were there any months where your income was significantly higher or lower than expected? How did this affect your budget?

Adjustments:

- If your income fluctuates more than expected, consider adjusting your budget to reflect these changes.
- Reallocate funds to different categories as needed.

Adjustment Needed	Reason	New Budget Allocation ($)
Ex. $ 300	*Groceries price increase*	*$ 800*
		$
		$
		$
		$
		$
		$

Step 4: Reflection

How effective was your budget in managing your irregular income?

___

___

___

Did you encounter any challenges, and how did you address them?

___

___

___

What changes will you make to improve your budgeting process in the future?

___

___

___

Step 5: Future Planning

How will you prepare for months with lower-than-expected income?

____

____

____

What strategies will you use to build a financial cushion for irregular income periods?

____

____

____

ACTIVITY 13: ORGANIZE YOUR REFLECTION

Impact Challenge: Create Your Teen Budget Binder

You've done the work; now it's time to organize it!

Put your budgeting and debt strategies into one personalized binder.

✏️ **Instructions:** Print or draw out the following:

- Your Monthly Budget
- Your Debt Repayment Plan
- Your Irregular Income Budget (if applicable)
    - Decorate a binder or folder. Make it your own with colors, labels, and motivational quotes.
    - Present your binder to your parent or mentor.

Include a "My Why" page: Why being debt-free and budget-conscious matters to you.

📣 **Conversation Starter:** Ask your parent(s) if they've used the Snowball or Avalanche method and what they learned from it.

Reflection: How does organizing your finances in a binder help your confidence? What did your family say about your budget?

CHAPTER 5
BUILDING AND PROTECTING WEALTH

Objective: Learn strategies to build wealth over time and protect your assets through proper planning.

ACTIVITY 14: ESTATE PLANNING CHECKLIST (PREPARE THIS WHEN LEAVING HOME!)

Task	Details	Target Deadline	Completion Date
Ex. Writing a Will	*Who will be my beneficiaries; write down who will be executor of my estate; allocations, etc.*	*8/15/XX*	*9/15/XX*
1. Write a Will	Specify your beneficiaries and executor.		
2. Set Up a Trust	Protect your assets and specify how they will be managed.		
3. Assign Power of Attorney	Designate someone to make legal decisions on your behalf.		
4. Designate a Healthcare Proxy	Appoint someone to make medical decisions for you.		
5. Organize Digital Assets	Inventory and manage your online accounts and passwords.		
6. Update Beneficiaries	Review and update beneficiaries for life insurance, retirement accounts, etc.		
7. Plan for Minor Children	Appoint guardians and set up funds for their care and education.		
8. Prepare Funeral Instructions	Specify your wishes for your funeral and burial/cremation.		
9. Review Your Estate Plan	Regularly review and update your estate plan to reflect life changes.		

Create your personalized estate planning checklist. Start with the easiest task, set deadlines for completion, and check off each task as you complete it.

Final Thoughts—Reflection

How did creating an estate planning checklist help you feel more prepared for the future? Did you feel overwhelmed because of the heavy length?

____

____

____

____

____

What was the most challenging part of this activity, and how did you overcome it? Do you feel more prepared to speak with a lawyer or want to become a lawyer?

____

____

____

____

____

ACTIVITY 15: TAX-EFFICIENT INVESTING STRATEGY

Research and list three tax-efficient investing strategies (e.g., using Roth IRAs, HSAs, or tax-loss harvesting). Develop a plan to implement one or more of these strategies in your own investment portfolio.

Strategy	Description	Potential Benefits	Applicability to My Portfolio
Tax Loss Harvesting	*Briefly describe the strategy and how it works.*	*List the potential tax savings and other benefits.*	*Assess whether this strategy fits your financial goals and portfolio.*
1.			
2.			
3.			
4.			
5.			
6.			

ACTIVITY 16: IMPACT CHALLENGE: WRITE YOUR WEALTH PROTECTION LETTER

Wealth isn't just about money—it's about mindset, values, and vision. Use this challenge to reflect on your goals and start shaping your legacy.

✏ **Instructions:** Write a short letter (one page max) to your future self or to your family.

Include:

- Why protecting your money is important to you.
- The steps you're taking now (saving, learning, planning).
- How your money will impact your life and others in the future.

🎯 **Optional:** Put the letter in an envelope labeled "Open in 5 Years." Or read it to someone who supports your journey.

📸 **Photo Challenge:** Share a snippet (quote or line) of your letter on social media or in a family group chat to inspire others.

Reflection: How did it feel to write this letter? What emotions came up as you imagined your future?

CHAPTER 6
EMBRACING FINANCIAL TECHNOLOGY

Objective: Explore the impact of technology on finance and how to leverage it for personal gain.

ACTIVITY 17: RESEARCH FINTECH TOOLS

Step 1: *Identify three fintech tools or apps that you are interested in exploring. These could be related to budgeting, investing, saving, or general financial management.*

Tool/App Name	Purpose	Notes
1. ABC	*Budgeting*	*I like how easy it is to add my expenses & income*
1.		
2.		
3.		

Step 2: *Explore and Test the Tools*

Instructions: Spend time exploring each tool. Sign up, if necessary, and test its features to understand how it works and how it could benefit your future.

Tool/App Name	Features Tested	Ease of Use (1-5)
1. ABC	*Budget tracking, alerts, etc.*	*4/5*
1.		___/5
2.		___/5
3.		___/5

Step 3: *Write Short Reviews*

Instructions: Write a short review for each fintech tool or app, covering the following aspects:

- **Overview:** Briefly describe the tool and its primary purpose.
- **Pros:** List the advantages or strengths of the tool.
- **Cons:** List any disadvantages or areas where the tool could be improved.
- **Usage:** Explain how you might use this tool to improve your financial management.

Tool/App Name: ____________________

Overview:

____

____

____

Pros:

____

____

Cons:

____

____

How I Might Use It:

____

____

____

Tool/App Name: ____________

Overview:

____

____

____

Pros:

____

____

Cons:

____

____

How I Might Use It:

____

____

____

Tool/App Name: ____________________

Overview:

____

____

____

Pros:

____

____

Cons:

____

____

How I Might Use It:

___

___

___

Step 4: *Compare the Tools*

Instructions: After reviewing each tool, compare them to determine which one(s) you find most useful.

Criteria	Tool/App 1	Tool/App 2	Tool/App 3
Ex. Ease of Use (1-5)	*5 (highest)*	*1 (lowest)*	*3 (Medium)*
Ease of Use			
Features			
Customizability			
Support/Resources			
Total Overall Rating			

Step 5: *Reflection and Future Exploration*

Self-Reflection

How did the exploration of these tools help you better understand your financial habits?

____

____

Are there any other tools you would like to explore in the future?

____

____

Future Exploration:

List any additional fintech tools or apps you might want to explore later.

______________ ______________ ______________

______________ ______________ ______________

______________ ______________ ______________

ACTIVITY 18: BLOCKCHAIN AND FINTECH APPLICATION

Objective: To explore how blockchain technology is being applied in the financial sector beyond cryptocurrencies and to analyze its potential impact on financial transactions or investments.

Instructions:

Step 1: Research Blockchain Applications

Investigate a real-world application of blockchain technology that is not directly related to cryptocurrencies. Examples include:

- **Smart Contracts**: Automated contracts that execute when predefined conditions are met, reducing the need for intermediaries.

- **Supply Chain Management**: Enhancing transparency and traceability in the supply chain, which can improve trust and efficiency.
- **Decentralized Finance (DeFi)**: Financial services provided on blockchain networks, offering alternatives to traditional banking.

Step 2: Select an Application for Detailed Study

Choose one specific application of blockchain technology that interests you and has significant implications for financial transactions or investments.

- Selected Application: ____
- Reason for Selection: ____

Step 3: Write a Brief Report:

In one to two pages, write a report on the selected application. Your report should include:

- **Introduction**: Briefly introduce the application and its relevance to the financial sector.
- **How It Works**: Explain how the technology operates, highlighting key features like security, transparency, and decentralization.

____

____

____

- **Impact on Financial Transactions or Investments**: Analyze how this technology could transform financial transactions or investments. Consider aspects like cost reduction, efficiency, security, and accessibility.

____

____

____

____

- **Potential Challenges**: Discuss any potential challenges or risks associated with this technology, such as regulatory issues, scalability, or adoption hurdles.

- **Conclusion**: Summarize the key points and reflect on the future potential of the technology in the financial industry.

ACTIVITY 19: TECH DEMO DAY FOR YOU AND YOUR FAMILY!

Let your inner tech expertise shine! This challenge is all about showing others how to use one of the financial apps or tools you like the most!

Instructions: Choose one fintech app (budgeting, investing, etc.) you tested.

Walk a parent or family member through:

- What it does
- Why you like it
- How it helps with money

Bonus Task: Help them sign up and explore the tool together. Explain the features step-by-step, like a tutorial.

Optional: Create a one-page review comparing the pros and cons of two to three apps and share it with your family.

Reflection: How confident did you feel explaining the tool? Do you think it helped your parent or friend? Would you recommend this app to others? If so, think about the value it created.

CHAPTER 7
SELF-EVALUATION AND YOUR FUTURE PLANS

Objective: Reflect on your progress and plan for continued financial education.

ACTIVITY 20: PERSONAL FINANCIAL PROGRESS EVALUATION

Review your financial progress over the course of this workbook. Write a reflection on what you've learned, how your financial habits have changed, and areas where you still want to improve.

Review Your Journey

Take some time to go back through the activities and exercises you've completed in this workbook. Consider how your understanding of financial topics has evolved and how your financial situation has changed.

Reflect on Your Learning

Write a reflection that addresses the following:

Key learning: What are the most important lessons you've learned throughout this workbook? How have these insights shaped your financial decisions?

____

____

____

____

Changes in financial habits: Describe any changes in your financial habits or behaviors. For example, have you become more disciplined with budgeting, started investing, or taken steps to reduce debt?

____

____

____

____

Challenges overcome: Reflect on any challenges you encountered during this process. How did you overcome them, and what did you learn from these experiences?

____

____

____

____

Assess Your Progress

Evaluate your current financial situation compared to where you started. Consider the goals you set earlier in the workbook and how close you are to achieving them.

Use the following questions to guide your assessment:

Have you reached any of your financial goals? If so, which ones?

What specific actions have contributed to your progress?

In what areas do you feel most confident, and where do you feel there is still room for improvement?

Identify Areas for Improvement

Based on your reflection and assessment, identify the areas where you still want to improve. This may include further refining your budgeting skills, increasing your savings rate, or gaining a deeper understanding of investing.

Outline steps you can take to continue making progress in these areas. Set one or two specific goals to focus on in the coming months.

Conclude your reflection with any final thoughts or feelings about your financial journey. What are you most proud of? How do you plan to stay motivated moving forward?

How has this workbook influenced your overall approach to personal finance?

____

____

____

____

What advice would you give to someone just starting their financial journey?

____

____

____

____

ACTIVITY 21: CONTINUING FINANCIAL EDUCATION PLAN

Create a plan to continue your financial education. This may include reading additional books, taking online courses, or setting up regular meetings with a financial advisor. List specific resources and set a timeline for completing them.

Review Your Journey

Take some time to go back through the activities and exercises you've completed in this workbook. Consider how your understanding of financial topics has evolved and how your financial situation has changed.

Reflect on Your Learning

Write a reflection that addresses the following:

Key Learning: What are the most important lessons you've learned throughout this workbook? How have these insights shaped your financial decisions?

____

____

____

____

____

____

ACTIVITY 22: PRESENT YOUR FINANCIAL GROWTH SNAPSHOT!

Impact Challenge: Present Your Financial Growth Snapshot because your journey is worth celebrating. Show how far you've come by creating a visual before-and-after snapshot.

Instructions: Create/use a two-column chart:

- Column 1: "Before I Started This Workbook"
- Column 2: "After Completing This Workbook"

Add statements comparing your thoughts, habits, or knowledge.

Display It: Turn it into a poster, journal page, or slideshow and present it to your family, teacher, or mentor.

Inspire Others: If you're comfortable, share your biggest lesson learned on social media, in a student group, group of friends, or with your bestie.

Reflection: What change makes you most proud of yourself? How will you stay on track with your financial goals moving forward?

Before I Started This Workbook	After Completing This Workbook

Before I Started This Workbook	After Completing This Workbook

FINAL REFLECTION: REFLECT, UPDATE, AND PLAN

Revisit Your Essay

Instructions: Begin by re-reading the essay you wrote at the beginning of this workbook. Reflect on your initial thoughts about your financial mindset, habits, and what you hoped to achieve. Consider how your understanding has evolved and how your goals may have changed.

Initial Reflections	Updated Reflections
Ex. "I've always struggled with managing my finances, often spending impulsively and failing to stick to a budget. My financial mindset has been mostly reactive when I deal with problems as they arise rather than planning ahead. I hope that by completing this workbook, I'll learn how to take control of my finances, develop better spending habits, and start saving consistently."	*Ex. "After working through this workbook, I've realized that my financial struggles stem from a lack of clear goals and planning. I've shifted from a reactive mindset to a proactive one, where I now prioritize setting realistic financial goals and tracking my progress regularly. I've started using a budgeting app to monitor my spending and have set up automatic transfers to build my savings. I feel more confident in my ability to manage my finances and am committed to maintaining these positive habits moving forward."*
1.	
2.	
3.	

Initial Reflections	Updated Reflections
4.	
5.	
6.	
7.	
8.	
9.	
10.	

UPDATE YOUR ESSAY

Instructions: After reflecting, update your essay to reflect on your current financial mindset, revised goals, and new financial habits. Be specific about what you plan to do differently moving forward.

Current Financial Mindset: Describe how your financial mindset has evolved.

Revised Financial Goals: Outline your updated financial goals based on your new insights. Plus, discuss your future aspirations and challenges.

New Financial Habits: Identify the habits you intend to cultivate to support your goals.

DEVELOP YOUR ACTION PLAN

Instructions: Break down your revised goals into actionable steps that you can take every week, three months, six months, and year. For each timeframe, include specific tasks, deadlines, and any resources you'll need to stay on track.

Weekly Action Plan

Week	Goal(s)	Tool/App 2	Resources Needed
Week X	*E.g., Improve budgeting*	*E.g., Review monthly expenses, set budget*	*Budgeting app, bank statements*
Week 1			
Week 2			
Week 3			
Week 4			
Week 5			
Week 6			

Three-Month Action Plan

Month	Goal(s)	Action Steps	Resources Needed
X	*E.g., Build an emergency fund*	*E.g., Set up automatic transfers to savings*	*Banking app, income statements*
Month 1			
Month 2			
Month 3			
Analyze & Plan for the next months!			

Six-Month Action Plan

Month	Goal(s)	Action Steps	Resources Needed
X–X	*E.g., Reduce debt by 10%*	*E.g., Increase payments using snowball method*	*Debt repayment plan, income*
Month 1			
Month 2			
Month 3			
Month 4			
Month 5			
Month 6			
Analyze & Plan for the next months!			

Yearly Action Plan

Year	Goal	Action Steps	Resources Needed
20XX	*E.g., Maximize retirement contributions*	*E.g., Review and adjust contributions to 401(k)*	*Financial advisor, retirement plan*
20____			
20____			
20____			
20____			
20____			
When Life Throws Curve Balls, Adjust Your Goals & Plans! Continue to Analyze & Track Your Progress.			

SET CHECK-IN POINTS

Instructions: Schedule regular check-ins to review your progress and make any necessary adjustments. These can be aligned with your weekly, three-month, six-month, and yearly goals to ensure you stay on track.

Check-In Date	Progress Review	Adjustments Needed
July 25, 20XX	*Completed weekly budget reviews; savings on track but overspending on dining out.*	*Reduce dining out budget by 10% and reallocate to savings.*

FINAL THOUGHTS

As you take the actionable steps in this workbook, remember that all this financial literacy learning is about reshaping your future! As a teenager, the financial decisions you make now will have a lasting impact on your life. Your self-discipline lays the groundwork for financial independence when you choose to save your money, do your own research before investing, and protect your money every day.

Since you know how to avoid debt traps and achieve your goals with the actions you take each day, this ripple effect will build confidence and give you the freedom to shape your future.

These actions won't just affect you. They will influence your future family's life, as well. When you master the skills of managing money, you'll be able to provide for your loved ones, offer financial security, and pass down the knowledge you've gained. Teaching future generations about money will help break cycles of financial stress and create a legacy of financial literacy and stability.

Remember, the path to your future success starts with your disciplined choices today. By fully embracing the principles in this workbook and staying dedicated to your financial growth, you're not just preparing for a life of prosperity—you are creating it. Each step opens the door to more extraordinary personal achievements and endless opportunities for your future family. This journey is lifelong, but the rewards are incredible, transforming your life and the legacy you'll leave behind!

ADDITIONAL RESOURCES

GREAT BOOKS TO READ

***Rich Dad Poor Dad* by Robert T. Kiyosaki**

- **Overview:** A classic personal finance book that contrasts the financial philosophies of Kiyosaki's "rich dad" and "poor dad."
- **Why Read:** Robert offers easy-to-read insights on how to build wealth through investing in real estate and entrepreneurship.
- **Link:** https://www.amazon.com/Rich-Dad-Poor-Teach-Middle/dp/1612680194/

***The Intelligent Investor* by Benjamin Graham**

- **Overview:** A foundational text on value investing, written by one of the most respected investment advisors of the twentieth century.
- **Why Read:** Teaches the importance of long-term investment strategies and the dangers of speculative behavior.
- **Link:** https://www.amazon.com/Intelligent-Investor-Definitive-Value-Investing/dp/0060555661/

***Simple Financial Wealth* by Growth Mindset Publishing (Chad K. Smith, MBA)**

- **Overview:** A comprehensive guide to managing finances, securing retirement, and transforming money into financial freedom. It covers saving, investing, credit improvement, tax-efficient strategies, and more to help readers build wealth.
- **Why Read:** Provides actionable steps for people looking to improve their financial health and retire with confidence, simplifying complex financial concepts for beginners.
- **Link:** https://www.amazon.com/dp/B0F4WFVKTS

WEBSITES

Investopedia

- **Overview:** A comprehensive resource for learning about financial terms, investment strategies, and market news.
- **Why Use:** Offers tutorials, articles, and tools for both beginners and advanced investors.
- **Link:** Visit Investopedia - https://www.investopedia.com/

NerdWallet

- **Overview:** A personal finance website that provides advice on credit cards, mortgages, insurance, and more.
- **Why Use:** Great for comparing financial products and getting practical tips on saving and investing.
- **Link:** Visit NerdWallet - https://www.nerdwallet.com/

The Financial Diet

- **Overview:** A blog and community focused on personal finance and lifestyle for young adults.
- **Why Use:** Offers relatable content on budgeting, saving, and financial planning.
- **Link:** Visit The Financial Diet - https://thefinancialdiet.com/

BUDGETING APPS

YNAB (You Need A Budget)

- **Overview:** A popular budgeting app that helps you allocate every dollar and build a strong financial foundation.
- **Why Use:** YNAB is known for its effective method of giving every dollar a job and improving financial habits.
- **Link:** Download YNAB - https://www.ynab.com/

Mint

- **Overview:** A free budgeting tool that automatically tracks your finances and categorizes expenses.
- **Why Use:** Mint is user-friendly and provides a comprehensive view of your finances in one place.
- **Link:** Download Mint - https://mint.intuit.com/

PocketGuard

- **Overview:** A budgeting app that helps you track your spending and see how much you have left to spend after bills and savings.
- **Why Use:** Great for those who want a simple overview of their finances with easy-to-understand visuals.
- **Link:** Download PocketGuard - https://pocketguard.com/

COURSES

"Financial Markets" by Yale University (Coursera)

- **Overview:** A course that provides an overview of the ideas, methods, and institutions that allow human society to manage risks and foster enterprise.

- **Why Take:** Taught by Nobel laureate Robert Shiller, it's a great introduction to the financial system.
- **Link:** Enroll on Coursera - https://www.coursera.org/learn/financial-markets-global

"Personal & Family Financial Planning" by the University of Florida (Coursera)

- **Overview:**A course focused on personal finance management, including budgeting, credit, taxes, and investing.
- **Why Take:** Offers practical knowledge for managing personal and family finances effectively.
- **Link:** Enroll on Coursera - https://www.coursera.org/learn/family-planning

"Learn financial literacy" by many Highly Ranked Universities!

- **Overview:** Financial literacy combines personal finance, financial concepts, and financial planning to help individuals build wealth and establish long-term stability.
- **Why Take:** Ideal for those interested in understanding the economic landscape in order to prepare for a better future.
- **Link:** Learn on edX - https://www.edx.org/learn/financial-literacy

"Compound interest is the eighth wonder of the world. He who understands it, earns it; he who doesn't, pays it."

ALBERT EINSTEIN

"It's not how much money you make, but how much money you keep, how hard it works for you, and how many generations you keep it for."

ROBERT KIYOSAKI

"You must gain control over your money, or the lack of it will forever control you."

DAVE RAMSEY

"The key to making money is to stay invested."

SUZE ORMAN

"Know what you own, and know why you own it."

PETER LYNCH

"The individual investor should act consistently as an investor and not as a speculator."

BENJAMIN GRAHAM

" Work like there is someone working twenty-four hours a day to take it all away from you."

MARK CUBAN

"If you never want to be criticized, for goodness' sake don't do anything new."

JEFF BEZOS

"The biggest adventure you can take is to live the life of your dreams."

OPRAH WINFREY

"When something is important enough, you do it even if the odds are not in your favor."

ELON MUSK

"The more you learn, the more you earn."

WARREN BUFFETT

"Sometimes by losing a battle you find a new way to win the war."

DONALD J. TRUMP

LET'S MAKE THAT MONEY CHECKLIST

☐ Babysitting or pet sitting
☐ Lawn care or yard cleanup
☐ Sell items on eBay, Mercari, or Facebook Marketplace
☐ Start a YouTube or TikTok channel with value-based content
☐ Create digital art, templates, or planners to sell on Etsy
☐ Offer tech support or tutoring for elders or neighbors
☐ Do odd jobs through TaskRabbit or local apps (with parental help)
☐ Wash cars or detail interiors
☐ Design logos or social media posts with Canva/Fiverr
☐ Create and sell your own merchandise (T-shirts, stickers, etc.)
☐ Offer grocery delivery or help with errands
☐ Launch a blog or podcast around your passion
☐ Offer music lessons if you play an instrument
☐ Monetize your skills: photography, video editing, gaming
☐ Partner with a friend to build a weekend hustle

GET IN CONTROL OF YOUR CASH CHECKLIST

☐ I know how much money I earn each month
☐ I track every dollar I spend for at least thirty days
☐ I created a simple budget for myself
☐ I use an app or spreadsheet to stay organized
☐ I know the difference between needs and wants
☐ I limit impulse purchases
☐ I set a weekly spending limit for fun stuff

☐ I'm building a savings habit (even if it's just $5/week)
☐ I review my spending habits monthly
☐ I understand the difference between a debit card and a credit card
☐ I talk to someone I trust when I'm unsure about a money decision

DISCOVER THE POWER OF MONEY

☐ I watched a video on how banks make money
☐ I know what compound interest is
☐ I understand inflation and why prices rise
☐ I learned the difference between gross pay and net pay
☐ I know what taxes are taken out of a paycheck
☐ I explored what credit is and how scores work
☐ I understand investing basics: stocks, bonds, mutual funds
☐ I learned how people make money with real estate
☐ I know what passive income is
☐ I looked up what entrepreneurs do
☐ I studied how the stock market works
☐ I found one financial podcast or YouTube channel to follow

STACK YOUR SAVINGS LIKE A PRO CHECKLIST

☐ I opened a savings account (with help if needed)
☐ I set a savings goal (ex: $100 in 3 months)
☐ I deposit a percentage of every dollar I earn
☐ I keep my savings separate from my spending money
☐ I track how close I am to my goal
☐ I avoid dipping into savings for impulse buys
☐ I use a jar or envelope system for visual saving
☐ I started a Dream Fund (travel, college, business, etc.)
☐ I challenge myself to save for 7 days in a row
☐ I use cash for fun purchases so I don't overspend
☐ I celebrate each milestone (with something free or fun)

BUDGET LIKE A BOSS CHECKLIST

☐ I list all the money I earn (allowance, jobs, gifts)
☐ I list all my regular expenses (lunch, gas, fun)
☐ I assign every dollar a job (Save, Spend, Give)
☐ I follow the 50/30/20 rule or a version that works for me
☐ I set a limit for weekly fun money
☐ I update my budget weekly or biweekly
☐ I include future savings in my budget
☐ I learned to adjust my budget when needed
☐ I reviewed my budget with a parent/mentor
☐ I plan for both short-term and long-term goals
☐ I use an app or printable to stay on track

PREPARE TO CRUSH CREDIT CHECKLIST

☐ I know what a credit score is and why it is important
☐ I know how a score is calculated
☐ I learned why missing payments hurts your score
☐ I researched the risks of debt and interest rates
☐ I understand how to use a credit card responsibly
☐ I avoid spending money I don't have
☐ I know how to check my credit score when I'm over eighteen
☐ I avoid payday loans and buy-now-pay-later traps
☐ I learned about student loans and repayment terms
☐ I understand the phrase: "Credit can help or haunt you."

VISUALIZE YOUR WEALTHY FUTURE CHECKLIST

☐ I created a vision board for my financial future
☐ I added pictures of the career or lifestyle I want
☐ I wrote three goals for the next twelve months
☐ I wrote three goals for the next five years
☐ I included money habits I want to stick to

- ☐ I shared my vision board with someone I trust
- ☐ I included inspiring quotes from money experts
- ☐ I keep my board visible (wall, notebook, screensaver)
- ☐ I update it every few months
- ☐ I added “Why I want to be financially free” in bold letters
- ☐ I believe I CAN build the life I imagine, and I update my vision board

YOUR $1,500 PIGGY SAVING $$ CHALLENGE STARTS NOW!

Instructions: Cut this out and put it on a shoe box to make a piggy saving bank! Each time you put in $50 or $100, cross it out. You cannot touch the money until they are all crossed out! This is also a discipline challenge, too. You got this!

CHALLENGE: Can you save $1,000 in 12 months? How about a FAMILY CHALLENGE to see who can save the most for the next vacation adventure!! Remember that life's a journey, not a destination. Enjoy your family, explore your intuition, be a constant learn, and no regrets!

$50

$50

$100

$100

$50

$100

$100

$50

REFERENCES

1. Personal & family financial planning. (2020, August 8). Coursera. https://www.coursera.org/learn/family-planning

2. Investopedia. "Investopedia." https://www.investopedia.com/

3. Mint. (n.d.). Budget Tracker & Planner | Free Online Money Management | Mint. Mint. https://mint.intuit.com/

4. NerdWallet. (n.d.). NerdWallet: Finance smarter. https://www.nerdwallet.com/

5. PocketGuard: Budgeting App & Finance Planner. (2025, June 25). PocketGuard | Your Personal Money & Bill Organizer. https://pocketguard.com/

6. The Financial Diet. (2022, July 6). Home - the financial diet. https://thefinancialdiet.com/

7. YNAB. (n.d.). https://www.ynab.com/

THANK YOURSELF!

👏 **Give yourself some serious credit!** You took real steps toward securing your financial future—and that's a big deal. You've proven that with the right moves, you *can* take charge of your money and build the life you desire. Keep that momentum going because your journey to financial freedom is just getting started. ✨ Mentor a friend or share do this workbook together to inspire someone else to level up, too!

Made in the USA
Monee, IL
14 September 2026

63093420R00059